HEAD AND SHOULDERS TOPS
THE ESSENTIAL FACTS

HEAD AND SHOULDERS TOPS

THE
ESSENTIAL FACTS

by

David Schwartz

and

Robin Griffiths

Burleigh Publishing Company

© Burleigh Publishing Company 1997

Published by Burleigh Publishing Company Ltd,
Burleigh Hall, Burleigh, Stroud, Gloucestershire GL5 2PF
First published 1997

ISBN 0 9523961 6 5

A CIP record for this book is available from the British Library

Printed in England by
Redwood Books, Trowbridge, Wiltshire

Notice

Whilst every effort has been made to ensure that information in this book
is correct, no liability can be accepted for any loss incurred in any way

CONTENTS

CHAPTER ONE – AFTER 100 YEARS, AN
      OVERNIGHT SENSATION   *page 1*

CHAPTER TWO – HOW WELL DO THEY WORK?   *page 9*

CHAPTER THREE – WATCH THE PRECEDING
      PRICE ADVANCE   *page 13*
Prior Dominant Low   *page 14*
Length of Preliminary Rally   *page 14*
Size of Preliminary Rally   *page 16*
Average Monthly Gain   *page 17*

CHAPTER FOUR – LEFT SHOULDER   *page 21*
Height of Left Shoulder   *page 21*
Height Relative to Height of Head   *page 23*
Height Relative to Pre-Formation Price Rise   *page 25*
Number of Weeks   *page 28*

CHAPTER FIVE – THE HEAD IS IMPORTANT   *page 31*
Height of Head   *page 32*
Price Rise from Prior Dominant Low   *page 33*
Head Height Relative to Right Shoulder
      Height   *page 36*
Number of Weeks   *page 38*

CHAPTER SIX – RIGHT SHOULDER   *page 41*
  Height of Right Shoulder   *page 41*
  Number of Weeks   *page 42*
  Symmetry between Left and Right Shoulders   *page 42*

CHAPTER SEVEN – LENGTH OF ENTIRE FORMATION   *page 47*
  Relative Width of Head   *page 48*
  Wait for Three Per Cent Confirmation   *page 50*

CHAPTER EIGHT – NECKLINE   *page 53*

CHAPTER NINE – WHAT TO EXPECT AFTER A VALID
    HEAD AND SHOULDERS   *page 55*
  Pre-Formation Rally   *page 55*
  Relative Width of Head   *page 56*
  Right Shoulder Width   *page 57*
  Odds of Large Fall Following Pull Backs   *page 57*

CHAPTER TEN – PULLING IT ALL TOGETHER   *page 63*

CHAPTER ELEVEN – CLOSING OBSERVATIONS   *page 67*
  Multiple Patterns   *page 67*
  Odd Shapes   *page 68*
  Volume   *page 70*
  Market Indices   *page 71*

FREE NEWSLETTER   *page 72*

ABOUT THE AUTHORS

DAVID SCHWARTZ

Stock market historian David Schwartz is well known for his research on key UK stock market trends that have affected investors for much of the twentieth century.

His regularly-updated *Schwartz Stock Market Handbook*, a valued reference tool for many investors, shows that the stock market is not nearly as random and unpredictable as some commentators suggest.

Schwartz frequently writes about long-running stock market trends in the leading weekend newspapers. His use of history to forecast the future is 'must' reading for many investors.

ROBIN GRIFFITHS

Robin Griffiths is Head of Technical Analysis at HSBC James Capel and is considered to be the City's top technical analyst.

He is a past President and now fellow of the British Society of Technical Analysts. He also was President of the International Federation of Technical Analysts for three years and is now on its Board of Directors.

Griffiths is regularly quoted in the financial press throughout the English- and Japanese-speaking worlds.

DISCLAIMER

This book is essentially a review of past stock market trends. It is based upon an historical analysis of closing prices for various publicly listed companies available at the time this book was prepared.

Every statement we make about possible future price movements is a statistical projection derived from past trends. No one knows if any of these relationships will continue in the future. Our observations are not intended to be recommendations to buy or sell any particular stock nor the market as a whole.

All statements about profits or losses associated with any buy or sell action are calculated before all fees or taxes.

Remember that the price of any stock market investment can go down as well as up. You can easily lose some or all of your investment. Be sure to discuss the risk of any investment with a qualified advisor before making any investment decision.

ACKNOWLEDGEMENTS

We are very grateful to Datastream for providing all charts. Special thanks go to Sarah Webb of Datastream, the best client service executive anyone could ever hope for.

CHAPTER 1
AFTER 100 YEARS, AN
OVERNIGHT SENSATION

In the stock market, as in other aspects of life, all good things eventually end. No company's share price continues to rise forever.

Spotting the right moment to sell is a critically important but difficult skill to master. Indeed, some commentators have humorously observed that there is a single common element linking every major stock market drop in history – no one saw it coming.

Happily, investors are not completely powerless in their effort to spot when it is time to sell. Technical analysts, or chartists as they are often called, use several different tools to help them to spot trend changes. As a group, these tools are known as reversal patterns.

Reversal patterns have become widely used in recent years but many have been in the public domain for decades. Charles Dow, editor of the Wall Street Journal at the beginning of the twentieth century and father of the Dow Jones Industrial Average wrote about them 100 years ago.

The best known of all reversal patterns is the head and shoulders formation. Investors have long been fascinated by this pattern, especially by its perceived ability to forecast the size of the price decline that follows.

As the Tarmac price trend reveals in Chart 1.1, there are four key components to a head and shoulders pattern:

■ There must be a sizeable run-up in share prices before the actual formation even begins to form. It is critically important to remember that head and shoulders tops are reversal patterns that are

TARMAC

Source: DATASTREAM

Chart 1.1: Tarmac peaked early in 1994, near the beginning of a bear market that hit UK shares by 18%. For most investors, the bear market was short-lived. Prices of the average share bottomed out in mid-year and soon began to rise. But Tarmac did not participate in the new bull market. Few technical analysts were surprised when Tarmac continued to fall in the second half of 1994 and most of 1995. The large price advance prior to the formation of the head and shoulders pattern, coupled with three well-formed price bubbles (points A, B and C), strongly suggested that Tarmac shares would remain weak in the months ahead.

followed by price drops reversing recent gains. In the absence of a sizeable pre-formation rise, there is nothing to reverse. Many pre-formation rallies found on daily price charts run for at least 12 months.

■ The end of the pre-formation advance is marked by a minor price dip as some investors take profits. Although it is not apparent at the time, the dip is actually the left shoulder of the formation (point A on Chart 1.1). Left shoulders usually form over a period of several weeks or months. There are wide differences in the height of left shoulders that are typically found on daily price charts although the average shoulder peaks 15% above its starting point. In this respect, Tarmac is slightly above average.

■ The left shoulder decline encourages new buyers to jump in, hoping for a continuation of the rally (point B). They push prices above the previous high, the top of the left shoulder. This new peak proves to be a temporary affair. Prices soon drift back down to the same general area where the left shoulder's decline ended. Sometimes this new low is exactly the same as the previous low. At other times, it is a bit higher, like Tarmac, or lower.

Chartists call this second price bubble the head of the formation. The point to which prices drop at the completion of the head is called the neckline. Draw a line connecting the final lows of the left shoulder and head and you will see why it has this name.

The typical head found on a daily price chart rises 30% above the neckline. But, once again, there are few patterns that are exactly average.

■ The final phase is the formation of the right shoulder, triggered by a third wave of buying that drives up prices once again. But this time, the rally peters out before prices reach the high point seen during the formation of the head (point C). By definition, the peak of the right shoulder must be lower than the height of the head or it is not a true head and shoulders pattern.

In theory, the completed formation is easy to spot. Unfortunately, there is a huge gap between theory and reality. Head and shoulders tops are among the most misdiagnosed and misinterpreted of all technical patterns.

If the pattern is of classic shape and symmetry, the task is simple enough. Unfortunately, real-world tops are rarely textbook perfect. Invariably, one shoulder is higher or wider than the other. The trend for T & N shows both of these tendencies, a relatively dominant left shoulder which is both wider and taller than its right shoulder opposite number (see Chart 1.2). Short-term gyrations often create double or triple shoulders. The head can rise well above either shoulder like Tarmac's or rise so little that it stands just a fraction above the left shoulder, like Hollas Group in Chart 1.3. Necklines are virtually always slanted, not horizontal. As these observations suggest, judgement is often required to spot this important reversal pattern and interpret it. This book will show you how to do both.

Once the formation runs its course, the ground is set for further large price declines. We say 'further' because the decline has already started at this point, the drop from the peak of the head to the end of the right shoulder. Chartists believe that the minimum distance prices will fall is equal to either the size of the rise from the prior dominant low to the start of the left shoulder or to the distance from the top of the head to the neckline on that day, whichever is smaller. This forecast of things to come is called the minimum price objective.

The truth of the matter is that head and shoulders patterns are not always followed by a price drop to the minimum price objective. However, the frequency with which these declines do occur has caused this chart tool to be treated as an important trend reversal pattern. In fact, its reputation as a price peak indicator has become so deep-seated that many investors mistakenly believe it *only* occurs at the peak of long-running rallies. As we shall soon see, this image is wrong. The pattern can occur anytime during the course of a broad up-move as well as at the end.

The reason for this inaccuracy is computer-related. Until recently, most equity price charts were drawn by hand on a daily or weekly

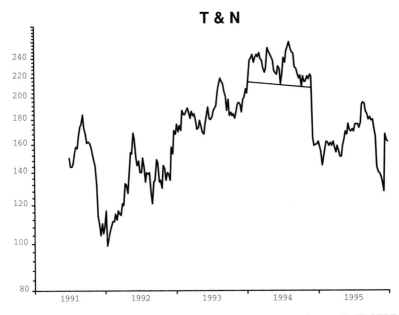

T & N

Source: DATASTREAM

Chart 1.2: Head and shoulders tops are rarely textbook-perfect. T&N's left shoulder has two bubbles and is much wider that the head or right shoulder. Its neckline slants and the right shoulder peak is much lower than the left shoulder peak. Nevertheless, prices fell quite sharply once the formation ran to completion. This book will help investors to spot head and shoulders tops that do not precisely fit the image of how they should look.

basis. Due to these relatively broad time frames, head and shoulders formations were often spotted near the end of a major multi-month price rise. This led to its reputation as a chart pattern that only appeared at the end of a lengthy price rise, a so-called major trend reversal indicator.

The use of computers changed many aspects of investing. Short-term traders began to chart price changes minute-by-minute. They discovered head and shoulders formations on their short-term charts

HOLLAS GROUP

Source: DATASTREAM

Chart 1.3: Hollas Group's left shoulder is much taller and narrower than its right shoulder. Its neckline is upward-sloping. But prices fell very sharply once the reversal pattern ran its course despite these flaws. Incidentally, our research finds that most necklines are upward-sloping, not horizontal like textbooks usually show. In other words, the Hollas Group neckline is the norm, not the exception.

as well as their long-term ones. Not surprisingly, they learned that price declines often followed these newly discovered chart patterns, with one major difference. There were fewer large price drops following short-term rallies so minimal that they were only visible on a minute-by-minute chart. The reason should be obvious. Without a large price run-up, there is little ground to reverse once the trend changes.

The purpose of this book is to help investors to use head and shoulders patterns to maximise profits. For this reason, we concentrate on formations from daily and weekly charts where completed patterns often signal a major trend change.

In theory, these formations are easy to recognise. But like many other aspects of investing, the devil is in the detail. In the real world, they are among the most frequently mis-diagnosed and mis-interpreted of all technical charting tools. Unfortunately, the cost of an error can be high, either encouraging investors to continue to hold shares when they should be selling, or encouraging them to sell too early and missing out on a solid price rise.

Our goal is to rectify this problem by providing lots of practical advice and actual examples of successful head and shoulders formations that precede large price drops.

In Chapter Ten, we provide a valuable set of guidelines to help investors to calculate the likelihood that any individual head and shoulders pattern they encounter will produce a large post-formation fall.

CHAPTER 2
HOW WELL DO THEY WORK?

According to chartist folklore, the *minimum* size of the fall that follows the completion of a head and shoulders formation may be estimated by measuring the smaller of a) the increase from the prior dominant low to the start of the left shoulder or b) the distance from the high point of the formation, the peak of the head, to the neckline directly below the peak. This spread is known as the 'minimum price objective'. In the case of Hollas Group (see Chart 1.3), the preliminary rally raised prices from around 11 to 23, a gain of 12. Soon after, the head peaked at 32 on a day that the neckline stood at 24, a spread of eight. This implies a minimum price decline of eight points once prices pierce the neckline of the right shoulder, which is exactly what happened.

Detractors claim that head and shoulders formations, indeed all reversal patterns, do not reliably predict trend changes or that they issue warning signals well *after* the fact, when it is too late to take advantage of the information.

Our goal was to evaluate the claims of each faction by locating a large, representative cross-section of head and shoulders patterns and measuring the size of each subsequent price drop. In view of the fact that all charting techniques do not work equally well in each of the world's financial markets, we deliberately limited our investigation to UK equity charts. The starting point was a review of share price trends of 500 leading UK companies from 1992 to the present listed in the Equity Chart Book, a monthly publication by Investment Research of Cambridge Ltd.

This research led to two critically important conclusions. Most important of all is that it validated what chartists have long claimed:

SIZE OF DECLINE FOLLOWING COMPLETION OF
HEAD AND SHOULDERS PATTERN

PERCENT OF MINIMUM PRICE OBJECTIVE	TOTAL
49% or less	28%
50–99%	32%
100% or more	40%

Table 2.1: Many head and shoulders formations are not followed by price drops that meet or exceed the minimum price objective. Fortunately, you can raise the odds of spotting winners due for a large fall. This book provides many clues.

head and shoulders tops are worth monitoring. Prices often do fall in the weeks and months that follow the completion of this reversal pattern. The simple truth is that the critics are wrong.

On the other hand, these reversal patterns do not work quite as well as proponents claim. According to our research, head and shoulders tops are far from flawless. Twenty-eight per cent of all completed patterns are followed by a price drop which is less than 50% of the minimum price objective predicted by chartist folklore, a significant failure rate (see Table 2.1).

Another 32% of all confirmed patterns are followed by price drops of 50–99% of the minimum price objective. In total, 60% of all formations are not followed by a decline that reaches its minimum price objective. Just 40% of all post-declines equal or exceed the minimum price objective.

But do not be too quick to reject the message of a head and shoulders top formation because of this failure rate. As shown in Table 2.2, most failed patterns produce little or no profit in the next 12 months. The vast majority could not even manage to rise above the peak of the right shoulder which is, typically, not much of a rise to look forward

WHERE PRICES STOOD 12 MONTHS AFTER COMPLETION OF HEAD AND SHOULDERS PATTERN

Patterns failing to produce price drops of sufficient size   60%

WHERE PRICES STOOD 12 MONTHS LATER

Below right shoulder neckline	23%
Neckline to right shoulder peak	11%
Above right shoulder peak to head peak	13%
Above head peak	13%

Table 2.2: The odds of a big price rise in the 12 months that follow a completed head and shoulders top are very low. Just 13% of all head and shoulders tops are followed by a strong rise in the year ahead. It is a powerful warning for those considering whether or not to invest in a company at what looks like a bargain price.

to over a 12-month period.

Just 13% of all examined patterns were followed by a rise in the next 12 months that propelled prices to a new high. In other words, there is little up-side potential for the next 12 months once a head and shoulders pattern forms, even if the price fails to drop as expected. It is an important point to consider whether you are a potential buyer or a seller. To our way of thinking, if you do nothing more than remember this single fact, you will soon justify the expense of this book many times over.

Fortunately, our research uncovered a number of ways to improve the odds of spotting the head and shoulders tops most likely to be followed by large declines that meet or exceed the minimum price objective. These winning patterns tend to have unique characteristics. The sections to follow will highlight these characteristics.

CHAPTER 3
WATCH THE PRECEDING
PRICE ADVANCE

A crucial problem often faced by analysts is deciding whether or not a chart candidate is a valid head and shoulders top. Subjectivity often enters into such debates. As we see things, subjectivity is fine for experts who have a proven track record and have earned the right to trust their judgement. But for most investors, intuitive feelings about whether or not the pre-formation price rise is sufficient, the left shoulder is large enough, or the whole formation 'feels right' is a recipe for disaster. Instead, we opted for a judgement-free system based upon these simple conditions:

■ Shares in the company being monitored had to be in a long-term up-trend. If the 200-day average was not rising at the time of a suspected formation, the pattern was rejected.

■ The suspected top area had to contain three separate and distinct price bubbles. After the peak of each bubble, prices had to return to a support area, what the chartists call a neckline.

■ The three bubbles could be any height or width just as long as the middle one (the head) was taller than the other two. The size of this height advantage was not material. A head that was just a fraction of one per cent above the other two bubbles qualified.

Using this judgement-free system, we isolated every price trend in the Equity Chart Book that fulfilled all three conditions. Each chart was studied intensively in order to identify variables associated with winning formations, that is, subsequent price drops that met or exceeded the minimum price objective.

Prior Dominant Low

Several variables well worth monitoring are associated with the pre-formation price rise, the rally preceding the start of the left shoulder. We start with the prior dominant low which marks the beginning of the pre-formation rally.

If the concept of a 'prior dominant low' is new to you, think of it as the low point from which the rally begins. It is usually quite easy to spot, typically at the end of a substantial sell-off. The Hollas Group and Glynwed bottoms in the second half of 1992 are good examples of a prior dominant low (see Charts 1.3 and 3.1).

The odds that a post-formation drop will meet or exceed the minimum price objective correlate with the share price at the start of the pre-formation rally or prior dominant low. As Table 3.1 shows, the higher the initial starting price, the higher the odds of a large post-formation decline. For price trends with prior dominant lows over 180, half produce large post-formation declines. Many of the 'failed' formations generate near misses, price declines in the 50–99% range. In contrast, just 34% of all formations that start off below 180 produce large post-formation declines. Many of the 'failures' produce price drops in the 15–45% range.

Length of Preliminary Rally

Another variable worth watching is the number of weeks it takes for prices to rise from their prior dominant low to the start of the left shoulder.

Two time periods are especially likely to produce large post-formation declines: very short rallies that raise prices to the left shoulder in less than 30 weeks, and rallies that run their course in 60–74 weeks. Glynwed International's climb over a period of 67 weeks is a

GLYNWED INTERNATIONAL

Source: DATASTREAM

Chart 3.1: The peak of Glynwed's head rose about 50 points above the neck-line, suggesting a target of at least 50 points on the down-side once the right shoulder was completed. This is exactly what happened. A number of clues tipped that Glynwed would decline by the expected amount including a prelimi-nary price advance of 88% that took 67 weeks to run its course, both good signs. Also important is the fact that the left shoulder was more than 70% as tall as the head. More on this in Chapter 4.

good example of a time frame that is often followed by a post-forma-tion drop that meets or exceeds the minimum price objective (see Chart 3.1). All other pre-formation time periods are associated with low odds of producing a post-formation price drop that meets or exceeds the minimum price objective (see Table 3.2).

LIKELIHOOD THAT POST-FORMATION DECLINE WILL MEET OR EXCEED THE MINIMUM PRICE OBJECTIVE

(ALL HEAD AND SHOULDERS PATTERNS)

SHARE PRICE AT PRIOR DOMINANT LOW	ODDS OF LARGE POST- FORMATION PRICE DECLINE
180 or under	34%
Over 180	51%

Table 3.1: Large post-formation price declines are less likely if shares are under 180 at the prior dominant low. Some long-term investors might be tempted to wait it out, especially if the height of the head bubble is low. But the odds of a substantial price rise in the year ahead are poor, not a very good reason for holding on.

SIZE OF PRELIMINARY RALLY

It also pays to monitor the size of the price increase between the prior dominant low and the neckline at the start of the left shoulder. Working with actual raw price data is unproductive but if you convert all price change data into percentages, interesting relationships appear.

The calculation is simple. Merely divide the price at the neckline which signals the beginning of the left shoulder, by the price at the prior dominant low and convert to a percentage. A rally that starts at 50 and first penetrates the neckline of the left shoulder at 125 would produce a price increase of 150%.

Research shows that large post-formation price drops that meet or exceed the minimum price objective often follow rallies that raise prices 70–89% above the prior dominant low. More than three out of four patterns that fit this profile produce large post-formation

LIKELIHOOD THAT POST-FORMATION DECLINE WILL MEET OR
EXCEED THE MINIMUM PRICE OBJECTIVE

(ALL HEAD AND SHOULDERS PATTERNS)

LENGTH OF PRE-FORMATION PRICE RISE	ODDS OF LARGE POST-FORMATION PRICE DECLINE
Under 30 weeks	55%
30–59 weeks	29%
60–74 weeks	71%
Over 74 weeks	28%

Table 3.2: The odds of a large post-formation price decline are especially high following a preliminary price run-up that runs its course in less than 30 weeks or in 60–74 weeks.

declines. Glynwed International is a good example of this trend in action. Its pre-formation rise of 88% was followed with a post-formation decline that well exceeded the minimum price objective (see Chart 3.1).

As Table 3.3 reveals, price shifts above or below the target range often produce failures, that is, tops not followed by a sufficiently large price drop.

AVERAGE MONTHLY GAIN

Another aspect of the preliminary rise, the average monthly price increase, is also worth watching. Here too, the calculation is easy to make. After computing the size of the increase from the prior dominant low to the neckline of the left shoulder in percentage terms, divide that figure by the number of months that the rally has run. For example, if a share started rallying from a prior dominant low of 50 to 125 at the start of the left shoulder neckline, over a period of 20

LIKELIHOOD THAT POST-FORMATION DECLINE WILL MEET OR EXCEED THE MINIMUM PRICE OBJECTIVE

(ALL HEAD AND SHOULDERS PATTERNS)

SIZE OF PRE-FORMATION PRICE RISE	ODDS OF LARGE POST-FORMATION PRICE DECLINE
Below 70%	28%
70–89%	77%
Over 89%	34%

Table 3.3: More than three-quarters of all head and shoulder tops preceded by a rally that raises prices 70-89% above the prior dominant low are followed by post-formation declines that meet or exceed the minimum price objective.

months, the average monthly price increase is a gain of 75 divided by the starting price of 50, or 150%, divided by 20 months or 7.5% per month.

There is an interesting correlation between the size of the average monthly increase and the odds of a post-formation decline that meets or exceeds the minimum price objective. Monthly price rises of 4.5–6.0% are most likely to produce large price drops following the successful completion of a head and shoulders formation.

The pre-formation rally by Glynwed International increased at a rate of 5% per month, still another signal that post-formation prices would fall by a sufficiently large amount. The price run-up for London and Manchester Group rose at an average rate of 6% per month during this same period (see Chart 3.2). As expected, prices fell sharply once the head and shoulders reversal pattern ran its course.

In contrast, pre-formation rallies outside the target range, because of either a more gradual or a steeper rise, are much less likely to be

LIKELIHOOD THAT POST-FORMATION DECLINE WILL MEET
OR EXCEED THE MINIMUM PRICE OBJECTIVE

(ALL HEAD AND SHOULDERS PATTERNS)

AVERAGE PRE-FORMATION MONTHLY PRICE RISE	ODDS OF LARGE POST-FORMATION PRICE DECLINE
Below 4.5%	19%
4.5–6.0%	60%
Over 6.0%	38%

Table 3.4: Price increases which rise within a range of 4.5–6.0% per month are most often associated with a post-formation decline that meets or exceeds the minimum price objective.

followed by a large price drop (see Table 3.4).

When using these trends, keep in mind that research for this book was based upon head and shoulders patterns that formed from 1992 to the present, a period with relatively short bull market rallies and bear market corrections. Overall stock market conditions obviously have an effect on the price trend of individual shares. The possibility exists that a long-running bull market like the one observed in the 1980s would alter some of these findings. But the concept of relatively moderate velocity outperforming more extreme readings is less likely to change.

LONDON AND MANCHESTER GROUP

Source: DATASTREAM

Chart 3.2: The pre-formation trend for London and Manchester Group raised prices for 60 weeks at an average rate of 6% per month. Both are good signs that the post-formation decline would meet or exceed the minimum price objective.

CHAPTER 4
LEFT SHOULDER

Many investors believe the height of the head is the single most important element of a head and shoulders formation to monitor. Our research shows that other elements are equally important.

Take the left shoulder for example. It is not common knowledge but the height and width of the left shoulder communicate important information about the size of the subsequent fall, once the formation is completed.

HEIGHT OF LEFT SHOULDER

By definition, a left shoulder peak must be lower than a head peak or it is not a valid head and shoulders formation.

The average left shoulder peaks 15% above the neckline on the day of the peak. More than 97% of all confirmed head and shoulders formations rise no higher than 39%. If a suspected formation produces a taller left shoulder, the odds are very high that the formation will not be completed, and no sell signal will be produced.

For trends that do develop into a confirmed head and shoulders top, experience shows that high odds of a large post-formation price drop go hand in-hand with left shoulders that are well-below average height.

The optimum height is a left shoulder that peaks 7.7–9.7% above the neckline. Hogg Robinson is a good example of such a price trend as it rose to 240 in late 1993, 8% above the neckline (see Chart 4.1). Large post-formation price declines occur about two-thirds of the time following left shoulder peaks within this range.

If the left shoulder peaks at a lower level, the odds of a large post-formation decline are about 50:50. The odds of a large decline are

HOGG ROBINSON

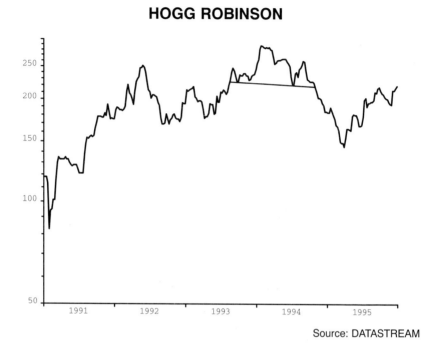

Source: DATASTREAM

Chart 4.1: Hogg Robinson's left shoulder peaked 8% above the neckline, comfortably within the 7.7% to 9.7% optimum target range. Another good sign is that the left shoulder is a very small proportion of the combined left shoulder/pre-formation price rise. Shares fell on cue once the formation ran its course.

worst of all when the left shoulder peaks more than 9.7% above the neckline (see Table 4.1).

To compute this relationship, divide the price at the peak of the left shoulder by the price at the neckline on that same day. If the left shoulder peak is 165 and the neckline price (which, of course, you will first be able to draw at a later date when the chart pattern is closer to completion) is 150, the height would be (165 – 150) ÷ 150 or .10. Move the decimal point two spaces to the right to convert the decimal to a percentage, in this case, 10%.

LIKELIHOOD THAT POST-FORMATION DECLINE WILL MEET
OR EXCEED THE MINIMUM PRICE OBJECTIVE

(ALL HEAD AND SHOULDERS PATTERNS)

HEIGHT OF LEFT SHOULDER ABOVE NECKLINE	ODDS OF LARGE POST-FORMATION PRICE DECLINE
Below 7.7%	52%
7.7–9.7%	65%
Over 9.7%	30%

Table 4.1: The best odds of a post-formation price drop that meets or exceeds the minimum price objective is when the left shoulder peaks 7.7–9.7% above the neckline.

HEIGHT RELATIVE TO HEIGHT OF HEAD

The relationship between the height of the left shoulder and that of the head carries another important warning signal. This indicator is calculated by dividing the height of the left shoulder from peak to neckline on the day of the peak, by the height of the head, also from peak to neckline. Assuming a left shoulder peak of 130 with a neckline reading of 100, and a head peak of 210 with a neckline reading of 110, the calculation would be $(130 - 100) \div (210 - 110)$ or $30 \div 100$ or 30%.

Research shows that the taller the left shoulder relative to the head, the higher the odds that the post-formation drop will meet or exceed the minimum price objective.

On the low end, formations with left shoulders less than 24% of the height of the head are often followed by small price drops once the formation is completed (see Table 4.2). Merely 12% meet or exceed the minimum price objective. With odds as low as this, some long-term investors might be tempted to hold on to their shares if the

LIKELIHOOD THAT POST-FORMATION DECLINE WILL MEET
OR EXCEED THE MINIMUM PRICE OBJECTIVE

(ALL HEAD AND SHOULDERS PATTERNS)

LEFT SHOULDER HEIGHT RELATIVE TO HEAD HEIGHT	ODDS OF LARGE POST-FORMATION PRICE DECLINE
Below 24%	12%
24–49%	35%
50–69%	46%
Over 69%	52%

Table 4.2: The taller the left shoulder relative to the head, the higher the odds that the post-formation price drop will meet or exceed the minimum price objective. Short left shoulders usually fail to produce large price drops.

chart pattern produced a relatively small head bubble. Before making that decision, remember that the possibility of a substantial price rise in the year ahead is also low.

The odds of a large decline steadily increase as the relative size of the left shoulder rises. At the opposite end of the range, left shoulder rallies that rise to at least 70% of the height of the head have a slightly better than 50:50 chance of being followed by a large post-formation price drop.

The Barclays Bank price trend (see Chart 4.2) provides a good example of this relationship. Prices doubled to over 600 after the UK left the ERM in 1992. The head and shoulders formation that followed produced a relatively tall left shoulder and a head that just managed to exceed the left shoulder peak. Post-formation prices fell as expected. Both Hollas Group and Glynwed (Charts 1.3 and 3.1) trends tell a similar story.

BARCLAYS

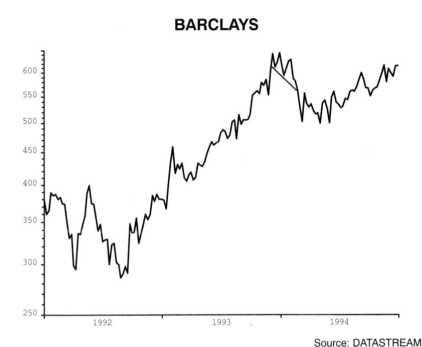

Source: DATASTREAM

Chart 4.2: The left shoulder that formed near the start of 1994 was a small portion of the total price rise from the prior dominant low to the left shoulder peak. At the same time, its height was 70% of the height of the head. Prices fell as expected once the formation was completed.

HEIGHT RELATIVE TO PRE-FORMATION PRICE RISE

Another height indicator worth monitoring is the relationship between the pre-formation run-up and the height of the left shoulder. We saw in the previous section that tall left shoulders (compared with heads) are a good sign. But the reverse is true when the left shoulder is compared to the pre-formation price run-up. Experience shows that relatively small left shoulders are most likely to produce large price declines once the formation is completed (see Table 4.3).

LIKELIHOOD THAT POST-FORMATION DECLINE WILL MEET OR EXCEED THE MINIMUM PRICE OBJECTIVE

(ALL HEAD AND SHOULDERS PATTERNS)

LEFT SHOULDER PORTION OF COMBINED LEFT SHOULDER/ PRE-FORMATION PRICE RISE	ODDS OF LARGE POST-FORMATION PRICE DECLINE
12% or less	65%
13–22%	41%
Over 22%	28%

Table 4.3: The smaller the left shoulder relative to the combined left shoulder/pre-formation price rise, the higher the odds that the post-formation price drop will meet or exceed the minimum price objective.

Before acting upon this relationship, first note that the height of the left shoulder is computed in a slightly different manner from the procedure shown earlier. For this indicator, it is necessary to measure height from the point the left shoulder first crosses the neckline at its beginning.

As an example, if a rally begins at the prior dominant low of 200, breaches the neckline to begin the left shoulder at 280 and reaches a left shoulder peak at 300, the calculation would be $(300 - 280) \div (300 - 200)$, or $20 \div 100$ or .20. As before, move the decimal point two spaces to the right to convert to a percentage, in this case, 20%.

Research shows that left shoulder rallies which are less than 12% of the combined height of the pre-formation and left shoulder rallies are most likely to produce big post-formation falls.

As the relative height of the left shoulder increases, the odds of a large post-formation drop decrease. Just one out of four formations with a left shoulder which occupies more than 22% of the combined pre-formation and left shoulder rally produce a large post-formation

KWIK SAVE GROUP

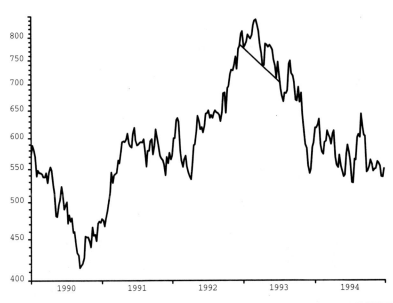

Source: DATASTREAM

Chart 4.3: Kwik Save's left shoulder occupied a small portion of the combined pre-formation/left shoulder rally and formed in less than five weeks. Both were good signs that the post-formation drop would be a large one.

drop once the entire head and shoulders formation runs its course.

Chart 4.3 provides a good example of the advantage of a large pre-formation rise relative to the height of the left shoulder. Notice how Kwik Save prices almost doubled as they moved from their prior dominant low in 1990 to the start of the left shoulder. Prices then rose about 30 points to the peak of the left shoulder, well within the target range. The post-formation decline was a large one, as expected.

Some readers may have noticed what seems like conflicting advice in the preceding sections. For example, the left shoulder peak in Chart 4.3 satisfies the need for a left shoulder to be a small portion

Likelihood that Post-Formation Decline Will Meet or Exceed the Minimum Price Objective

(All Head and Shoulders Patterns)

Weeks to form left shoulder	Odds of large post- formation price decline
5 weeks or less	60%
6–7 weeks	47%
8 weeks or more	26%

Table 4.4: Quick-forming left shoulders have the greatest likelihood of being followed by large price drops.

of the combined pre-formation/left shoulder price rise. At the same time, it is much shorter than the head, which is an undesirable characteristic. The simple truth is that real-world head and shoulders patterns are rarely perfect. They typically provide both positive and negative clues and it is up to the analyst to sort things out. Do not be disheartened. We will provide very useful advice on the subject of conflicting advice in Chapter 10.

NUMBER OF WEEKS

The length of time required for the left shoulder to form, from when it first rises above the neckline to the moment it returns to the neckline, is the final left shoulder indicator worth monitoring. Research finds that 60% of all left shoulders completed within five weeks are eventually followed by price drops that meet or exceed the minimum price objective (see Table 4.4).

Slower-forming left shoulders taking more than five weeks to form are less likely to produce a solid subsequent price drop. If the left shoulder takes eight or more weeks to form, the chance of a large

BRITISH AEROSPACE

Source: DATASTREAM

Chart 4.4: The pre-formation rally in British Aerospace shares eased into a lengthy head and shoulders top. One warning signal that post-formation prices might not decline to the minimum price objective was a very wide left shoulder which took nine months to form. Another point of concern was the left shoulder's height which occupied 37% of the combined pre-formation/left shoulder rally.

post-formation price drop is just 26%. British Aerospace is a good example of this trend in action (see Chart 4.4). Its price trend formed a left shoulder through much of 1993. The post-formation price drop that followed was virtually non-existent, more a continuation of a trading range plateau than a true decline.

CHAPTER 5
THE HEAD IS IMPORTANT

Experience shows that heads come in a very large variety of different shapes and sizes. By definition, the peak of the head must be higher than the peak of the left and right shoulder or the formation is not a valid head and shoulders reversal pattern. Aside from this critically important condition, there are no constraints on head shape or size. Virtually any shape is acceptable.

Research finds that the peak of the typical head rises 30% above the neckline. For lower-priced shares with head peaks no higher than 430, 98% have a head height of 8–72% above the neckline. If you are monitoring a potentially promising head and shoulders formation with a head height outside this range, there is little chance that it will develop into a valid formation.

For higher priced shares that peak over 430, 98% have a head height of 10–51% above the neckline. Here too, if you are monitoring a potentially promising formation with a head height outside this range, experience suggests there is a very small chance that it will eventually develop into a valid formation and deliver the expected price decline.

There is widespread belief that the head height, from neckline to peak, predicts the size of the subsequent fall. According to the commonly used rule of thumb, the distance prices are expected to fall once they slip below the neckline, known as the 'minimum price objective', is equal to or greater than the height of the head from neckline to peak.

As we have seen, this perception is often not supported by the facts. The chance of success is much lower, 40% to be precise. However, there are many ways to increase the odds of spotting for-

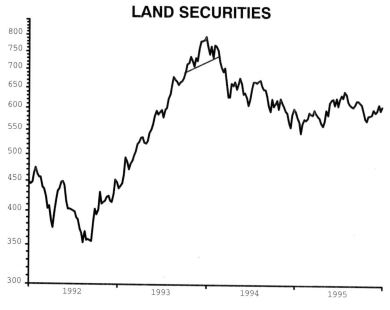

LAND SECURITIES

Source: DATASTREAM

Chart 5.1: The degree to which the head rises above the neckline often tips whether or not the post-formation price drop will meet or exceed the minimum price objective. Land Securities' head peaked about 12% above the neckline, well within the target range, a strong clue that the post-formation drop would be a large one.

mations that produce large subsequent drops. Several have already been discussed. Here are some more relationships worth monitoring.

HEIGHT OF HEAD

A good start point is to calculate the height of the head by subtracting the price at its peak from the price at the neckline on the same day. Divide this figure by the neckline price. A neckline price of 300 and peak price of 360 would produce a height reading of 20%.

LIKELIHOOD THAT POST-FORMATION DECLINE WILL MEET OR EXCEED THE MINIMUM PRICE OBJECTIVE

(ALL HEAD AND SHOULDERS PATTERNS)

HEIGHT OF HEAD	ODDS OF LARGE POST-FORMATION PRICE DECLINE
16.4% or less	79%
16.5–24.7%	40%
24.8–44.3%	28%
44.4% or more	8%

Table 5.1: More than three out of four heads that peak no higher than 16.4% above the neckline are followed by sizeable falls that meet or exceed the minimum price objective. This level of success drops sharply as the height of the head increases.

More than three out of four heads that rise no higher than 16.4% above the neckline are followed by a sizeable fall that meets or exceeds the minimum price objective. Land Securities illustrates this point with a late-1993 peak near 800, about 12% above its neckline. Prices fell sharply throughout 1994, as expected (see Chart 5.1).

Table 5.1 illustrates how the likelihood of success drops sharply as the height of the head increases. Just 8% of all head and shoulders patterns with heads that peak 44.4% or more above the neckline are followed by a large post-formation price drop.

PRICE RISE FROM PRIOR DOMINANT LOW

It also pays to monitor the size of the price run-up from the prior dominant low point to the peak of the head (see Table 5.2). To calculate this relationship, divide the price rise from the prior dominant

LIKELIHOOD THAT POST-FORMATION DECLINE WILL MEET OR EXCEED THE MINIMUM PRICE OBJECTIVE

(ALL HEAD AND SHOULDERS PATTERNS)

SIZE OF INCREASE FROM PRIOR DOMINANT LOW TO HEAD PEAK	ODDS OF LARGE POST-FORMATION PRICE DECLINE
113% or less	34%
114–144%	70%
145–212%	29%
213–250%	63%
251–349%	30%
350% or more	7%

Table 5.2: Two pockets of profitability to watch for are price rises of 114–144% and 213–250%. The odds of a large decline are much lower if the rally from the prior dominant low is outside either of these two ranges. Be especially careful if the rally is very strong. Price rises of 350% or more above the prior dominant low are rarely followed by large post-formation price drops.

low to the peak of the head by the price at the prior dominant low. By way of example, if prices rose from a prior dominant low of 80 to a head peak of 180, the calculation would be (180 − 80) ÷ 80 or 1.25. Move the decimal point two places to the right to convert to a percentage, in this case, 125%.

Research finds that price rises within a range of 114–144% and 213–250% are associated with above-average odds of a large post-formation price decline that meets or exceeds the minimum price objective. In both cases, the chance of a large decline is well over 50:50.

On the other hand, very large rallies that raise prices more than 250% above the prior dominant low are unlikely to produce a post-

TAYLOR WOODROW

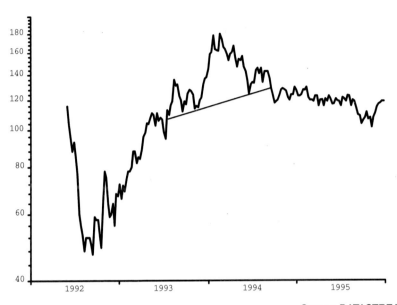

Source: DATASTREAM

Chart 5.2: In the rally that followed the UK's departure from the ERM, Taylor Woodrow's share price rose more than 250% from its prior dominant low to its head peak, an early danger signal. Another warning signal was the height of the head, about 50% above the neckline. Not surprisingly, the post-formation decline was disappointing.

formation price drop that meets or exceeds the minimum price objective. As the Taylor Woodrow price trend shows in Chart 5.2, such rises are simply too much good news. The rise from under 50 in 1992 to a peak of 180 gave investors a profit of over 250% and the post-formation price decline that followed was disappointing. WPP's trend in Chart 5.4 is another example of a strong price rise followed by a small decline.

LIKELIHOOD THAT POST-FORMATION DECLINE WILL MEET
OR EXCEED THE MINIMUM PRICE OBJECTIVE

(ALL HEAD AND SHOULDERS PATTERNS)

HEIGHT OF RIGHT SHOULDER RELATIVE TO HEIGHT OF HEAD	ODDS OF LARGE POST-FORMATION PRICE DECLINE
25% or less	19%
26–61%	33%
62–79%	57%
80% or more	77%

Table 5.3: The odds of a large post-formation decline are quite high if the right shoulder is at least 80% as high as the head. Smaller right shoulders are more likely to produce small post-formation declines.

HEAD HEIGHT RELATIVE TO RIGHT SHOULDER HEIGHT

Another relationship to watch is the height of the right shoulder relative to the head.

This indicator is calculated by dividing the rise of the right shoulder from neckline to peak, by the height of the head, also from neckline to peak. Assuming a right shoulder peak of 130 with a neckline reading of 100 on that same day, and a head peak of 210 with a neckline reading of 110, the calculation would be $(130 - 100) \div (210 - 110)$ or $30 \div 100$ or .30. Once again, convert to a percentage by moving the decimal point two spaces to the right, in this case, 30%.

Our research finds that relatively small right shoulders are often followed by small post-formation falls that do not meet or exceed the minimum price objective. Conversely, relatively tall right shoulders are more likely to be followed by a large drop.

Source: DATASTREAM

Chart 5.3: The right shoulder's height is quite low when compared with the head. In addition, the formation took well over one year to form. Both of these characteristics are often associated with small post-formation declines and British Land followed the norm.

As shown in Table 5.3, when the right shoulder is no more than 25% of the height of the head, the odds of a large post-formation drop are less than one in five. At the other extreme, when the right shoulder is at least 80% the height of the head, more than three out of four are followed by large post-formation price drops.

Chart 5.3 shows the price trend for British Land which rose sharply from its mid-1992 low to a January 1994 peak near 450. Unfortunately, the right shoulder's height was a small proportion of the head's height and the subsequent price drop did not reach the minimum price objective.

LIKELIHOOD THAT POST-FORMATION DECLINE WILL MEET OR
EXCEED THE MINIMUM PRICE OBJECTIVE

(ALL HEAD AND SHOULDERS PATTERNS)

NUMBER OF WEEKS FOR HEAD TO FORM	ODDS OF LARGE POST-FORMATION PRICE DECLINE
Less than 5 weeks	88%
5–14 weeks	60%
More than 14 weeks	17%

Table 5.4: Watch for heads that form in four weeks or less. The odds of a large post-formation decline are very high following fast-forming heads.

NUMBER OF WEEKS

The final variable to monitor is the length of time required for the head to form. Quick-forming heads are most likely to produce large post-formation price drops, especially those that form within five weeks. At the other extreme, heads that form in 14 weeks or longer are often not followed by subsequent falls that meet or exceed the minimum price objective. Fewer than one in five succeed (see Table 5.4).

WPP (see Chart 5.4) provides a good example of a well-formed head and shoulders top with one fatal flaw, a slow-forming head. Another example is the very wide head formation produced by British Land (see Chart 5.3)

One word of warning to investors who are itching to jump the gun following the development of a left shoulder and head. More than 90% of all formations that look like a left shoulder and head never develop into a fully-fledged head and shoulders format so resist the temptation to take any action based upon a partially completed signal.

Source: DATASTREAM

Chart 5.4: A number of warning signals suggested WPP's 18 month-long 'topping out' formation would not be followed by a large post-formation price decline. The left shoulder formed over a period of six months. The head peaked more that 400% above the prior dominant low. At its high point, it stood 44% above the neckline and took about six months to form.

CHAPTER 6
RIGHT SHOULDER

The final phase of a head and shoulders reversal pattern is the formation of the right shoulder. As in the case of the two earlier price bubbles, it is often triggered by a fresh wave of buy orders. But this time, buying pressure is much weaker and the rally ends before prices reach the high point of the head. By definition, the right shoulder peak must be lower than the head peak or it can not be classed as a head and shoulders pattern.

We touched on right shoulders in the previous chapter by noting that shoulders almost as tall as heads are likely to produce large post-formation price drops. Here are a few additional issues to consider.

HEIGHT OF RIGHT SHOULDER

A good starting point for a right shoulder evaluation is to measure its height.

Calculate height by subtracting the price at the neckline directly below the peak from the price at the peak, and divide by the neckline reading. A neckline price of 200 and peak of 230 would produce a height reading of $(230 - 200) \div 200$ or 0.15. Move the decimal point two places to the right to convert to a percentage, in this case, 15%.

The typical right shoulder rises 13% from neckline to peak, slightly lower than the average left shoulder. Research finds that 99% of all confirmed patterns produce a right shoulder that rises no more than 42% above the neckline. This statistic has important practical implications. If you are monitoring a potentially promising formation with a higher right shoulder, experience suggests low odds that it will develop into a valid formation.

LIKELIHOOD THAT POST-FORMATION DECLINE WILL MEET
OR EXCEED THE MINIMUM PRICE OBJECTIVE

(IF RIGHT SHOULDER PEAKS ABOVE 200)

NUMBER OF WEEKS FOR RIGHT SHOULDER TO FORM	ODDS OF LARGE POST-FORMATION PRICE DECLINE
Less than 5 weeks	66%
5–6 weeks	57%
7 weeks or more	20%

Table 6.1: For right shoulders that peak above 200, the faster it forms, the higher the odds of a large post-formation price decline.

NUMBER OF WEEKS

For right shoulders that peak above 200, our research finds that quick-forming shoulders are associated with high odds of a post-formation decline that meets or exceeds the minimum price objective (see Table 6.1). Look for right shoulders that run their course in five weeks or less. Chart 6.1 shows the price trend for Heywood Williams which rose sharply during 1993 and peaked in the first quarter of 1994. The head and shoulders pattern formed quite quickly, especially the right shoulder, and prices then fell quite sharply as expected.

In contrast, right shoulders that peak above 200 and form in seven weeks or longer have very low odds (one in five) of being followed by a large decline. No comparable trend exists for right shoulders that peak below 200.

SYMMETRY BETWEEN LEFT AND RIGHT SHOULDERS

Many investors expect head and shoulders patterns to have symmetrical left and right shoulders in terms of height and width. In fact, once a tentative neckline is drawn to connect a possible left shoulder

HEYWOOD WILLIAMS

Source: DATASTREAM

Chart 6.1: Quick-forming right shoulders are often followed by large post-formation declines that meet or exceed the minimum price objective. Heywood Williams is a good example with a right shoulder that formed in less than five weeks. On the other hand, the low height of the right shoulder peak relative to the head is a point of concern. Chapter 10 provides good advice on how to resolve the problem of conflicting signals.

and head, some chartists even project the height of the right shoulder peak by drawing a line that is parallel to the neckline, extending from the top of the left shoulder. During periods of stock market weakness, they gamble by selling or buying puts when prices approach their estimate of where the right shoulder will top out.

It is a risky practice to follow. Only 14% of all confirmed head and shoulders patterns have a right shoulder that is within 10% of the

PILKINGTON

Source: DATASTREAM

Chart 6.2: Symmetry is pretty to look at but not very useful when it comes to head and shoulders tops as the Pilkington chart shows. Another concern was the length of time required for the formation to run its course. Not surprisingly, the post-formation decline was disappointing.

height of the left shoulder. By way of example, a left shoulder that peaks 20% above the neckline would require a right shoulder peak within a range of 18–22% above the neckline to fit our definition. Even worse, such symmetrical patterns are not very likely to be followed by a decline that meets or exceeds the minimum price objective. Our investigation found that just 27% of all symmetrical right shoulders (those within 10% of the height of the left shoulder) produced a post-formation price drop that met or exceeded the minimum price objective.

Research into the relative width of the left versus right shoulder also produced disappointing results for symmetry fans. The length of time it takes for a left shoulder to form carries no clue about the length of time it will take for a right shoulder to form. Just 55% of all formations have left and right shoulders that run their course within four weeks of each other. The remaining formations are equally divided into two groups with the right shoulder either taking much more or much less time to form. So don't get lulled into a false sense of security because the left shoulder formed slowly and you expect similar right shoulder behaviour.

Most important of all, formations with similar left and right shoulder widths have the same odds of a large post-formation decline as asymmetrical formations. Pilkington's price trend is a good example of a pattern that is reasonably symmetrical in terms of left versus right shoulder height and width. However, the post-formation price drop failed to meet or exceed the minimum price objective (see Chart 6.2).

Clearly, symmetry is not worth seeking out.

CHAPTER 7
LENGTH OF ENTIRE FORMATION

Charting theory is full of untested myths. Some turn out to be quite accurate after being independently tested. But many are just partially true, based upon a useful premise but undermined by a glaring weakness or danger that makes their value suspect. Occasionally a myth is encountered that is completely incorrect. A good example is the myth of long-forming head and shoulders tops.

According to the myth, the longer it takes for a formation to complete, the more important its implications. Patterns that evolve over a period of many months or years are thought to be the springboard for bigger price falls compared with similar shaped patterns condensed into smaller time frames.

Our research shows conventional wisdom to be completely wrong. We find that the less time it takes for the formation to run its course, the more likely that the subsequent drop will meet or exceed the minimum price objective.

Among patterns extending for 18 weeks or less, 68% met or exceeded their post-formation minimum price objective. For longer-running formations, success was less likely. The worst performers were formations that took 43 weeks or longer to complete. Just 17% were followed by a large post-formation price drop (see Table 7.1).

Pilkington and Singer & Friedlander Group (see Charts 6.2 and 7.1) are examples of long-running chart patterns which failed to deliver large post-formation price declines despite the fact that they were preceded by large price run-ups.

When using this data, remember that our research was done during the 1990s, a period of mainly rising prices with occasional short, sharp corrections like in the Summer of 1992 and Spring of 1994. The

Likelihood that Post-formation Decline Will Meet
or Exceed the Minimum Price Objective

(All Head and Shoulders Patterns)

Number of Weeks for Entire Pattern to Form	Odds of Large Post-formation Price Decline
18 weeks or less	68%
19–27 weeks	52%
28–42 weeks	32%
More than 42 weeks	17%

Table 7.1: The odds of a large post-formation price drop are highest for fast-forming formations. The longer the pattern takes to form, the lower the odds that a large price drop will follow.

possibility exists that a different set of underlying stock market conditions could change the precise definition of these time frames.

Another issue worth considering is that we worked from daily price charts. Charts using longer or shorter time frames might reveal other head and shoulder patterns not apparent to us or hide some that we were able to identify. Tampering with our source material might change some conclusions as well.

Still, the underlying conclusion that shorter time periods are more likely to be followed by falls that meet or exceed the minimum price objective should hold true, no matter what type of chart is used.

RELATIVE WIDTH OF HEAD

Pay special attention to heads that take up 48–56% of total formation running time, in other words, heads that run for about half of the length of the total formation. Among heads of this relative length, any

SINGER AND FRIEDLANDER

Source: DATASTREAM

Chart 7.1: It took more than a year for Singer and Friedlander to complete its head and shoulders top. In addition, the relationship between the total formation width and the head issued its own warning signal. As expected the subsequent price decline was weak.

short-running formation that runs in its entirety for 27 weeks or less is very likely to be followed by a large post-formation price drop that meets or exceeds the minimum price objective. But if the total for mation runs for more than 27 weeks, the chance of a large post-formation price drop is just 11% (see Table 7.2).

Singer and Friedlander provides a good example of this phenomenon. After a sharp run-up triggered by our departure from the ERM, their shares drifted into a 58-week-long head and shoulders top with the head taking up half of this period, or 29 weeks. As expected, a

Likelihood That Post-Formation Decline Will Meet or Exceed the Minimum Price Objective

(Head Length of 48–56% of Total Pattern Length)

Number of Weeks for Entire Pattern to Form	Odds of Large Post-Formation Price Decline
27 weeks or less	82%
28 weeks or more	11%

Table 7.2: If the head width occupies around half the total formation time, big declines often follow a formation that runs to its entirety in 27 weeks or less.

very small price drop followed the completion of the formation (see Chart 7.1).

If the head occupies less than 48% of total formation running time, the precise odds of success change but the same general principle holds. Faster-running formations yield the best profit odds (see Table 7.3).

Wait for Three Per Cent Confirmation

Once a head and shoulders formation is completed, experience suggests that prices must drop at least 3% below the right shoulder neckline before the pattern can be officially confirmed.

Many investors are tempted to take action as soon as the right shoulder forms without waiting for the 3% confirmation signal. It is a risky policy to follow. Our research finds that in 27% of all apparently valid formations, prices do not drop 3% below the neckline. The Carlton Communications price trend shown in Chart 7.2 eventually touched the neckline at the tail-end of the right shoulder but failed to penetrate it decisively. Head and shoulders sellers were completely wrong-footed as prices rose, despite the fact that stock market conditions were generally poor during the fourth quarter of 1994 and first

CARLTON COMMUNICATIONS

Source: DATASTREAM

Chart 7.2: It pays to take no action until a post-formation decline reduces prices by at least 3% below the right shoulder neckline. About one out of four apparently valid formations behave like Carlton Communications and fail on this final and crucial test.

quarter of 1995. It vividly illustrates the importance of waiting for a 3% confirmation signal.

LIKELIHOOD THAT POST-FORMATION DECLINE WILL MEET OR EXCEED THE MINIMUM PRICE OBJECTIVE

(HEAD LENGTH LESS THAN 48% OF TOTAL PATTERN LENGTH)

NUMBER OF WEEKS FOR ENTIRE PATTERN TO FORM	ODDS OF LARGE POST-FORMATION PRICE DECLINE
27 weeks or less	65%
28–49 weeks	57%
More than 49 weeks	20%

Table 7.3: For short-running heads, the length of time occupied by the complete formation and the likelihood of a big post-formation price drop go hand-in-hand. Fast-forming patterns are more likely to be followed by a large drop than are slow-forming patterns.

CHAPTER 8
NECKLINE

Some investors imagine the typical head and shoulders top rests upon a horizontal neckline. As our many illustrations suggest, this image is inaccurate. In fact, only 14% of all confirmed head and shoulders tops rest upon a horizontal neckline so don't be too quick to ignore potential candidates because the neckline slopes.

We wondered if our definition of 'horizontal' was too rigorous and completed a series of experiments to test this concern.

■ When our definition of horizontal was changed to include all necklines that were precisely horizontal as well as those that rose or fell slightly, up to 0.5% per month, the number of horizontal necklines increased to 30%. A slope of this magnitude is bigger than you might think. Hogg Robinson's neckline (Chart 4.1) slopes downward at a rate of 0.5% per month.

■ When the definition was further broadened to include all necklines that rose or fell as much as 0.75% per month, fewer than one half of all necklines could be called horizontal, 43% to be precise.

The evidence is quite clear. Despite the fact that most investors think head and shoulders formations usually rest on a horizontal neckline, such patterns are in the minority.

Research shows that two-thirds of all necklines (65%) rise to the right, known as upward sloping necklines, and 21% fall to the right, known as downward sloping necklines.

Pilkington and Singer & Friedlander Group are good examples of upward slopes while Hogg Robinson is a downward example (see

Likelihood that Post-formation Decline Will Meet or Exceed the Minimum Price Objective

(ALL HEAD AND SHOULDERS PATTERNS)

Direction of slope	Odds of large post-formation price decline
Downward slope	53%
Horizontal slope	37%
Upward slope	34%

Table 8.1: The odds of a large post-formation price drop is significantly higher when the slope drops down to the right.

Charts 4.1, 6.2 and 7.1).

The probability of a post-formation price drop that meets or exceeds the minimum price objective is significantly higher when the slope is down than when it is horizontal or upward (See Table 8.1). Worst profit odds of all are provided by upward slopes which produce large post-formation price drops just 34% of the time.

CHAPTER 9
WHAT TO EXPECT AFTER A VALID
HEAD AND SHOULDERS

Once a head and shoulders pattern has successfully formed and prices drop below the neckline by at least 3%, chartists believe a very important sell signal has flashed and the stage is set for a further price drop.

Recall that the minimum price objective is equal to either a) the distance from the peak of the head to the neckline on the day of the peak or b) the total price run-up of the pre-formation rally from the prior dominant low to the start of the left shoulder, whichever is smaller. In other words, investors should expect a small price decline if a pattern with great potential is preceded by a very small pre-formation price run-up.

But before rushing to take any action, consider this surprising fact uncovered by our research: the post-formation drop is not always immediate. Prices pull back to the neckline or even rise above it about half the time before dropping to their final low. There are several ways to increase the odds of correctly forecasting if an individual price trend will pull back to the neckline, giving investors a second chance to sell (or in some cases, a better selling price) before the final drop begins.

PRE-FORMATION RALLY

One useful clue is the size of the price gain from the prior dominant low to the start of the left shoulder. Calculate this figure using the procedures described earlier.

LIKELIHOOD THAT POST-FORMATION DECLINE WILL PULL BACK
TO NECKLINE BEFORE FINAL FALL

(ALL HEAD AND SHOULDERS PATTERNS)

SIZE OF RISE FROM PRIOR DOMINANT LOW TO START OF LEFT SHOULDER	ODDS OF A PRICE PULL BACK
Below 69%	42%
69–89%	78%
90% or more	46%

Table 9.1: If prices rise within a range of 69–89% between the prior dominant low and the start of the left shoulder, the odds are high that a pull back to the neckline will take place once the formation is complete.

Research finds that price rises within a range of 69–89% above the prior dominant low are most likely to be followed by a pull back to the neckline once the formation is complete. The chance of shares pulling back to the neckline before resuming their fall are more than three out of four within this segment (see Table 9.1).

Gains above or below this range are much less likely to be followed by a post-formation pull back to the neckline.

RELATIVE WIDTH OF HEAD

Another way to spot formations likely to pull back to the neckline prior to the final drop is to measure the length of time taken for the head to form.

If the head occupies 34–60% of total formation time, the formation is unlikely to pull back to the neckline before starting its final decline. All other formations have a stronger chance of doing so before starting their final descent (see Table 9.2).

LIKELIHOOD THAT POST-FORMATION DECLINE WILL PULL BACK
TO NECKLINE BEFORE FINAL FALL

(ALL HEAD AND SHOULDERS PATTERNS)

SHARE OF TOTAL FORMATION TIME TAKEN BY HEAD	ODDS OF A PRICE PULL BACK
Below 34%	67%
34–60%	42%
61% or more	70%

Table 9.2: If the head takes 34–60% of total formation time, the odds are low that the completed formation will pull back to the neckline before starting its final decline.

RIGHT SHOULDER WIDTH

It also pays to monitor the number of weeks required for the right shoulder to form. Research finds that shoulders forming in seven to nine weeks are most likely to be followed by a pull back before the final decline begins. In contrast, fewer than half of very short- or very long-forming right shoulders are followed by pull backs (see Table 9.3.)

General Accident formed its right shoulder in 10 weeks (see Chart 9.1) and prices continued to drop as expected once the right shoulder was breached, without returning to the neckline.

ODDS OF LARGE FALL FOLLOWING PULL BACKS

If prices do pull back to the neckline or rise above it before the final drop, there are two factors that do a good job of tipping whether the subsequent fall will meet or exceed the minimum price objective.

One useful indicator is the number of weeks required for the full

LIKELIHOOD THAT POST-FORMATION DECLINE WILL PULL BACK TO NECKLINE BEFORE FINAL FALL

(ALL HEAD AND SHOULDERS PATTERNS)

NUMBER OF WEEKS TO FORM RIGHT SHOULDER	ODDS OF A PRICE PULL BACK
Less than 7 weeks	45%
7–9 weeks	68%
10 or more weeks	46%

Table 9.3: Right shoulders that form in seven to nine weeks are most likely to be followed by a pull back before the final decline begins.

head and shoulders pattern to form. Research shows that 82% of all head and shoulders patterns that form in less than 25 weeks and pull back to the neckline are followed by a large price drop that meets or exceeds the minimum price objective. The longer the formation takes to complete, the smaller the chance of a large drop following the pull back (see Table 9.4).

A final indicator to monitor is the height of the head above the neckline. As before, subtract the share price at the neckline directly below the peak, from the peak price, and divide by the neckline price. A neckline price of 300 and peak price of 360 would produce a height reading of $(360 - 300) \div 300$ or 20%.

Research finds that formations with very low head heights that pull back to the neckline are very likely to be followed by large price drops that meet or exceed the minimum price objective. The higher the head height, the lower the chance of a large drop following a pull back (see Table 9.5).

Head heights of 17% or less are often followed by large price drops once the pull back runs its course.

Hazlewood Foods produced a head that rose 15% above the neck-

GENERAL ACCIDENT

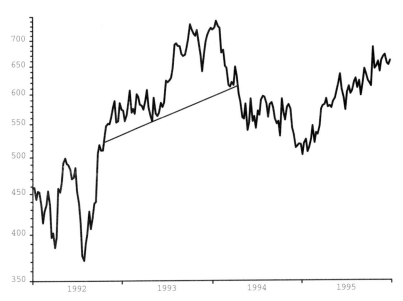

Source: DATASTREAM

Chart 9.1: General Accident follows the norm in one important respect. The odds of a price pull back before the final post-formation price decline are less than 50% if the right shoulder forms in less than seven weeks or more than 10 weeks.

line in Chart 9.2. A rise of this magnitude revealed nothing about the likelihood of a post-formation bounce-back before the final fall. But once that pull back did occur, the 15% head height signalled very high odds that a subsequent fall would probably deliver a large price drop. This is exactly what occurred.

Likelihood that Post-formation Decline Will Meet or Exceed the Minimum Price Objective

(Patterns that Pull Back to Neckline)

Number of weeks to form entire pattern	Odds of large post-formation price decline
Less than 25 weeks	82%
25–36 weeks	56%
37 or more weeks	19%

Table 9.4: Head and shoulders patterns that form in less than 25 weeks and pull back to the neckline are very likely to be followed by a large price drop.

Likelihood that Post-formation Decline will Meet or Exceed the Minimum Price Objective

(Patterns that Pull Back to Neckline)

Head height	Odds of large post-formation price decline
17% or less	89%
18% or more	33%

Table 9.5: Formations with head heights of 17% or less above the neckline that pull back to the neckline upon completion are usually followed by large price drops that meet or exceed the minimum price objective.

HAZLEWOOD FOODS

Source: DATASTREAM

Chart 9.2: It is difficult to forecast if or when a pull back to the neckline will occur. But once the pull back occurs, several indicators can tip which 'pull back formations' are more likely to be followed by a large decline. Hazlewood Foods' relatively low head height suggested that its pull back to the neckline would be followed by a large post-formation price drop that met or exceeded the minimum price objective.

CHAPTER 10
PULLING IT ALL TOGETHER

The preceding chapters provided several dozen different relationships that do a good job of forecasting whether or not a large post-formation price drop will occur.

Unfortunately, the real world is not a perfect place and neither is the stock market. The messages provided by different signals sometimes conflict with each other. A well-shaped left shoulder or head of appropriate width might send one message while a quirk in the right shoulder trend might be sending a completely different one. The purpose of this section is to help investors to balance such conflicting signals.

This chapter links many of the relationships that have already been reviewed into an accurate forecasting system. Our goal is to improve forecasting accuracy by using the sum total of all available evidence.

The forecasting sytem works as follows. A candidate head and shoulders top should be evaluated on each of the 14 dimensions listed in Table 10.1. For each of the 14 dimensions, award your candidate a specified number of points based upon the unique characteristics of the chart pattern being studied.

For example, if the prior dominant low of the chart pattern being studied is over 180, that pattern would accumulate three points. If the pre-formation rise extended for 100 weeks, the formation would accumulate two points. Using the point allocations of Table 10.1, rate the candidate formation on each of the 14 dimensions.

In case you are wondering, the point system is based upon a simple premise: the more likely an individual characteristic is associated with a large post-formation decline, the higher the number of

Weighting Procedure to Calculate Odds that Post-formation Decline Will Meet or Exceed Minimum Price Objective

PRIOR DOMINANT LOW	Weight	HEAD	Weight
Price: 180 or under	2	Height above neckline:	
Over 180	3	16.4% or less	4
PRE-FORMATION RISE		16.5–44.3%	2
Length:		44.4% or more	1
Under 30 weeks	3	Rise from prior dominant	
30–59 weeks	2	low to head peak:	
60–74 weeks	3	113% or less	2
Over 74 weeks	2	114–144%	3
Size:		145–212%	2
Under 70%	2	213–250%	3
70–89%	3	251–349%	2
Over 89%	2	350% or more	1
Average monthly rise:		Height of right shoulder	
Below 4.5%	1	relative to head:	
4.5–6.0%	3	25% or less	1
Over 6.0%	2	26–61%	2
LEFT SHOULDER		62–79%	3
Height above neckline:		80% or more	4
9.7% or less	3	Length:	
Over 9.7%	2	Less than 5 weeks	4
Height relative to head height:		5–14 weeks	3
Below 24%	1	More than 14 weeks	1
24–69%	2	**ENTIRE PATTERN**	
Over 69%	3	Length:	
Left shoulder part of combined left		27 weeks or less	3
shoulder/ pre-formation height:		28–42 weeks	2
12% or less	3	More than 42 weeks	1
Over 13%	2	Direction of neckline:	
Length:		Downward slope	3
5 weeks or less	3	Horizontal slope	2
6 weeks or more	2	Upward slope	2

Table 10.1: This important chart is easy to use. Assign the designated number of points to the head and shoulders pattern being analysed on each of the 14 factors listed here. Then add the total number of points. The higher the total, the more likely that a large post-formation price drop will follow. See Table 10.2 for specific odds of success.

POST-FORMATION DECLINE FORECAST

	14-FACTOR POINT TOTAL FROM TABLE 10.1			
	38 or more	32–37	29–31	Below 29
PERCENTAGE OF MINIMUM PRICE OBJECTIVE EXPECTED IN POST-FORMATION DECLINE				
100% or more	91%	48%	18%	3%
50–99%	3%	44%	44%	41%
49% or less	6%	8%	38%	56%

Table 10.2: Use this table to calculate whether the head and shoulders top being monitored is likely to be followed by a large post-formation price decline. For example, if the 14 factors from Table 10.1 produce a point total of 38 or higher, refer to the first column of the table which shows that there is a 91% chance that the post-formation price drop will meet or exceed the minimum price objective. At the other extreme, if the 14 factors from Table 10.1 produce a point total of 29 or less, refer to the fourth column which shows that the odds of a big drop are just 3% if the point total is below 29. Even worse, most of the failures miss by a large margin. More than half of all formations associated with a low point total subsequently decline by less than 50% of the minimum price objective.

points. You may want to refresh you memory on how to compute each of the 14 dimensions by returning to the appropriate chapter.

After evaluating the candidate formation on all 14 dimensions, total the number of points. Then refer to Table 10.2 which provides accurate odds on the likelihood that the subsequent post-formation decline will meet or exceed the minimum price objective.

CHAPTER 11
CLOSING OBSERVATIONS

MULTIPLE PATTERNS

Head and shoulder patterns have the capacity to frustrate investors who are new to this tool. One of the most frequently mentioned problems is that an investor looks at a chart, spots several different head and shoulders patterns and immediately begins to feel insecure about which is the 'real' one or the 'best' one.

The fact of the matter is that head and shoulders patterns can pop up several times on the same chart and even as an insert within a larger head and shoulders pattern. None is better or worse than the others. Each carries a message and it is up to the analyst to interpret it using the insights provided by this book.

Take the British Land price trend (see Chart 11.1) for example. It contains two necklines. Neckline A was discussed in an earlier section of this book. The width of the total formation provided a clear warning that the post-formation price decline might not meet the minimum price objective. This, of course, is what happened.

We now add neckline B to the chart, producing a smaller and considerably different head and shoulders top pattern. A completely new set of computations is now needed to forecast the odds of a large post-formation price drop (from a new starting point), and the minimum size of that drop.

A similar story is provided by the price trend for Heywood Williams in Chart 11.2. Neckline A supports a smaller, more powerful pattern. Neckline B portrays a different set of characteristics. Both formations carry an important message. It is your job to interpret each message, not wonder if one is better than the other.

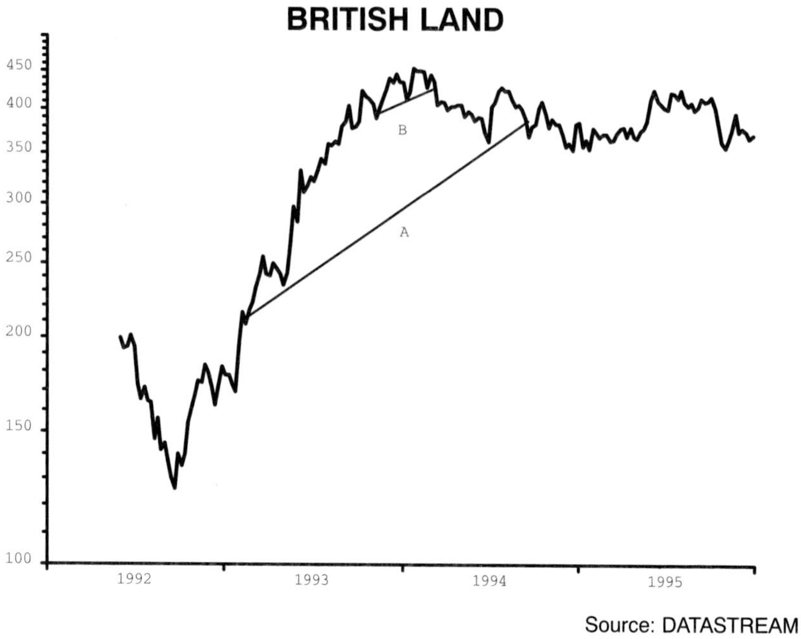

BRITISH LAND

Source: DATASTREAM

Chart 11.1: There is no such thing as a single best head and shoulders pattern. Each carries its own message. It is up to the analyst to interpret it. As shown earlier, neckline A suggests low odds of a large post-formation price decline. Two problems were the width of the entire formation and the low height of the right shoulder relative to the head. Neckline B, on the other hand, is a completely different pattern with different characteristics.

ODD SHAPES

Our analysis focused solely on classically-shaped head and shoulders formations featuring a single head and one shoulder on each side. But many valid head and shoulder formations have odd shapes that do not follow the norm. In addition to small patterns that form within the head of a larger formation, variations include two or more left shoulders, multiple heads, and two or more right shoulders or

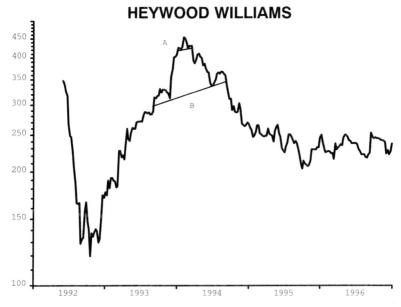

Source: DATASTREAM

Chart 11.2: The small size of the formation resting upon neckline A and the narrow right shoulder were positive signs for Heywood Williams and post-formation prices fell, right on cue. But the formation resting on neckline B tells a different story. Its width is much greater, as is the dominance of the head and the significantly larger minimum price objective. Once again, A and B tell different stories. But one is not better than the other.

various combinations of the three

   We were unable to locate enough examples of odd shaped patterns to conduct a reliable statistical analysis of their success rate. Several analysts have written that basic, or classically shaped patterns trigger post-formation declines that drop faster and further. Odd-shaped or complex patterns are said to drop more leisurely and drift horizontally more often.

   We report this information, without comment.

VOLUME

Accurate volume data is potentially a valuable tool for interpreting head and shoulders formations. Until recently, volume data for many listed companies was not readily available to private UK investors. As a result, our analysis of head and shoulders patterns omits any reference to volume.

Things are beginning to change. Several data suppliers have begun to provide volume figures for every listed company on a daily basis, for a fee. If you are monitoring the price trend for one of the larger companies, a free source is the back page of the Financial Times which lists yesterday's volume for many large companies.

American analysts who have easier access to daily volume figures for most listed companies report that average daily volume is typically heavier during the rising phase of the left shoulder and head, and lighter during the down phase.

They also report that volume patterns often change as the right shoulder runs its course. It is considered to be a very good sign if volume fails to rise on the up-slope of the right shoulder and rises significantly as prices begin to slide toward the neckline.

We cannot veryify these assertions via our own independent experiments and we report their claims without comment. If US volume trends do act in the way American analysts claim, we assume that UK head and shoulders patterns have similar tendencies but can not verify it through our own objective experimentation.

If you do have access to accurate daily volume data, remember that volume can be hard to interpret accurately because of its erratic nature. A steady pattern of 20,000 shares traded per day can suddenly shift to a one-day spurt of 300,000 and the analyst is left with the task of deciding if the one-day figure is a valid sign of volume explosion or if a single institution made a single trade which has less significance.

The best approach is to tally volume on a daily basis and compute a daily average for all trading days during the up-phase of each shoulder and head individually. Do the same for each down-phase.

Judgement is sometimes required. If a one-day 'volume spike' occurs, volume that is 10, 20 or 30 times heavier than normal, check with your broker or the financial press for clues. Was new information publicised? Was it an active day for other companies in the sector as well? Or did a single large buyer or seller cause much of the surge? If you decide that a single transaction was responsible for much of the activity, you may wish to ignore that day's volume as you compute your average. On the other hand, if there are several daily volume spikes, don't be too quick to ignore them. Common sense suggests that if lightning repeatedly strikes the same spot, there is usually a good reason.

MARKET INDICES

Another group of patterns we could not evaluate because of an insufficient sample size are head and shoulders tops involving broad market indices. Several UK stock market analysts have reported that head and shoulders tops are not effective predictors when applied to the UK stock market as a whole. We report their opinions without comment.

Free Newsletter

Free copies of the *Schwartz Stock Market Newsletter* are available to readers of this book. Each issue focuses on the three months ahead and contains our forecast of where the UK stock market is heading. See the insert following this page for further information.